DONALD J. TRUMP'S
Imperial Presidency
EXPOSED
through Rhyme

Poems by Valerie Luhman Anderson
Cartoons by Arnie Bermudez

Donald J. Trump's Imperial Presidency
EXPOSED Through Rhyme

Published by Wheatmark®
2030 East Speedway Boulevard, Suite 106
Tucson, Arizona 85719 USA
www.wheatmark.com

ISBN: 978-1-62787-834-0 (paperback)
ISBN: 978-1-62787-835-7 (ebook)
LCCN: 2020915064

Bulk ordering discounts are available through Wheatmark, Inc.
For more information, email orders@wheatmark.com
or call 1-888-934-0888

Linda,
Read and enjoy!
Your lifelong friend,
Valerie L Anderson

Contents

Cartoons

ACKNOWLEDGMENTS

As I began to explore publication of my poems, I joined a local writer's group to advise me. I owe much to the Savage Writers, whose astute review/comment of poems I shared has been most encouraging. I give them my heartfelt thanks and gratitude. The Savage Writers, which carries the surname of its founding member, meets weekly at a mid-town Tucson church and welcomes all with an interest in writing. Some members are published authors; others are pursuing novels, short stories, and memoirs.

Further acknowledgement goes to:

A Very Stable Genius, by Carol Leonnig and Phillip Rucker (See Health Hazards Ahead, Mental (un)Fitness—Ignorant, Illiterate)

Art of the Deal, by Tony Schwartz (See Tumpty's MO, 'I Take No Responsibility')

Commander-in-Cheat, by Rick Reilly (See All the President's Lies! Par-for-the-Course)

Trump Nation: The Art of Being Donald, by Trump biographer Timothy O'Brien (See The Cult of Trumpty, Hijacking the GOP)

Arizona Daily Star and syndicated cartoonist and columnist, David Fitzsimmons, for his personal encouragement and drawings that inspired a couple poems (See The Great Divide, Foreign Policy Fiasco—troops pulled from Syria, and Health Hazards Ahead, Physical (un)Fitness—Trump's annual exam by his White House physician)

Washington Post cartoonist, Ann Telnaes, 'Trump's Lynching' (See Impeachment Travails, Pre-impeachment Scuttle)

Acknowledgement also to authors whose literary works found their way into my poems:

Hans Christian Andersen—*Fairy Tales: The Emperor's New Clothes*

L. Frank Baum—*The Wonderful Wizard of Oz*

Lewis Carroll—*Through the Looking-glass*

Miguel De Cervantes—*Don Quixote de la Mancha*

Emily Dickinson—*I'm Nobody! Who Are You?*

Washington Irving—*The Legend of Sleepy Hollow*

'Mother Goose'—*Humpty Dumpty, The Old Woman Who Lived in a Shoe*

Edgar Allan Poe—*The Fall of the House of Usher, The Raven*

William Shakespeare—*Julius Caesar, Macbeth*

Dylan Thomas, Wales—*Do Not Go Gentle into that Good Night*

INTRODUCTION

I never set out to publish a book. As a former English teacher and career technical writer/project manager living in Tucson, AZ, I was having fun in retirement posting Trumpty poems as comments to articles in the digital *New York Times* (NYT) and Washington Post (WAPO).

I, like so many others, felt deep dismay the morning after the November 2016 election on hearing Donald Trump would become our next President. How could that have happened? Surely the Access Hollywood tapes and the nefarious financial dealings I'd read about would doom his presidential run. Wouldn't voters see that? I was wrong. I began posting comments—my small part, perhaps as protest—in 2017 with submission of a limerick to NYT on the confirmation of Scott Pruitt as Secretary of the Environmental Protection Agency (EPA). I felt good about getting my thoughts out on someone confirmed for a key administrative position who may not represent my interests. See appendix for poem.

I posted comments/poems under the moniker of VLA (my initials) in the NYT and under TucsonTransplant in WAPO. Why this form of 'protest'? My lifelong interest in music (choral and keyboard), language and design brought to bear the intricate interplay of rhyme and meter that make up the structure of a poem. Poetry has a musical quality, often employing 'pick up' beats (an eighth note) to a longer (quarter) note—taDUH. There are also 'dotted' rhythms (long, followed by short, as in DUHta). Most of my verses are iambic (metric unit/'foot') tetrameter (four stressed syllables). The poems flow lyrically, or as replies to comments have noted, 'scan' well. Add a little satire, and I had the perfect Trumpty poem.

My poems cover whatever was 'Breaking News': Trump's historic visit to North Korea, immigration, NRA and gun control, Mueller's report, impeachment, 2020 election prospects, Trump's zigging and zagging on decisions, his mangled rhetoric, and so much more! I wrote several poems on the Coronavirus fiasco of leadership. See Virus Crisis!

In compiling my book, I try to cite the relevant article's headline verbatim in a poem's introduction but paraphrase what other sources reported. I can't claim with complete accuracy that a poem is a posting match with a particular article, but I made my best determination. Given limited time to get this book out, I did not see a need to contact either paper for publishing records.

With the NYT, I found early on that submissions opening with 'Trumpty Dumpty' were possibly being flagged, especially when the same posting in WAPO (which doesn't require a review process) was getting several 'recommends' from readers. I then began substituting 'Donald J Trump' as an opening with better results. The Times did not accept all submissions, but for the purposes of this book, I included poems not posted, along with what may have been corresponding articles.

A few of the poems have no article citation. In those cases, the poem was too general to identify a particular article, or I simply wrote an 'introductory' verse; as in Health Hazards Ahead—Mental (un)Fitness, describing Trump's many sociopathic characteristics.

As my planning progressed, I contacted a cartoonist to bring some of the poems to life, and Arnie Bermudez, a local (Tucson) talent, much in demand, came on board. I told him I'd take as many as he was willing to do, given his full-time job doing animations and a looming 2020 election. The cartoons are interspersed throughout the book.

Arnie's cover illustration is based on the iconic poem, *The Emperor's New Clothes*. I adapted that poem in a way that pretty much sums up our President. See poem on back cover.

I invite you to read and enjoy these poems, and in noting the news that prompted them, it is my hope you will reflect on/replay the events that have defined and will define this Presidency.

I.

THE CULT OF TRUMPTY

Hijacking the GOP

Retro News: (2016) GOP abandons conservative principles in deference to Trump, who becomes their vehicle to regain power; Trump diehards declare war on those in GOP who don't go along, threatening to wreak havoc on their Senate and House races

> *When Trumpty Dumpty took control,*
> *The GOP lost its soul.*
> *He stole their dignity and pride,*
> *Taking them on a dangerous ride.*
> *The Grand Old Party is not the same,*
> *Now that they play Trumpty's game.*
> *Trumpty demands that they do as he says,*
> *But they'll pay a price for supporting this Prez.*

Corollary

Re: Article—(WAPO) 'The Center of the Orbit,' endangered Republicans go all-in on Trump (2/1/20)

> *When Trumpty Dumpty took control,*
> *The GOP lost its soul.*

The Party won't cross him; they fear for their job,
They give him a pass when he acts like the Mob.
Demand fealty—it's what Trump expects,
Wake up, Repubs, before the train wrecks.

Re: Article—(NYT) 'Sadness' and disbelief from a world missing American leadership (4/23/20)

Trumpty is a charlatan,
It's a Presidency he should not have won.
Our guard was down and he stole the show,
Helped by the Russians—that we know.
The Electoral College failed US all,
And what we have left is a wrecking ball.

Re: Article—(WAPO) New disclosures about lewd Trump video reveal his mastery of the GOP (7/10/19); other news sources: Trump's misconduct as revealed in 'Hollywood Access' tape failed to impact the 2016 election; Trump went on attack to survive, calling on belief that 'life has only winners and losers'; also, 'eat or be eaten'* *Trump biographer Timothy O'brien See also Health Hazards Ahead—Mental (un)Fitness, Manipulative

Trumpty proves how impunity,
'Has penetrated the GOP.'
Republican stooges do Trumpty's bidding,
And think it's okay, but who are they kidding?
Voters, I plead for the sake of our nation,
Please put an end to this deep infestation.

Re: Article—(WAPO) Praise for the Chief: Trump's Cabinet tells him it's an 'honor' and 'blessing' to serve (6/12/17); other news sources: CNN, Trump just held weirdest Cabinet meeting ever; (WAPO) The GOP traded its conservative principles for conservative judges (6/30/20)

Trumpty Dumpty gathers his staff,
Some dread how long this meeting might last.
They're expected to give effusive praise.
Do these esteemed members exist in a daze?
Watch them as they each take a turn,
Fawning remarks make our stomachs churn.
Some members seem to hold back somewhat,
They don't want to tell Trump what he is not?
An exception is Mattis—brave soul is he,*
He praises, instead, our military.
Why this undying support? The answer's not hard,
Tax cuts and judges are their due reward.

*James Mattis, Secretary of Defense

The 'Chosen One'

Re: Article—(WAPO) Why Christian Nationalists think Trump is heaven-sent (3/20/20); other news sources: USA Today, Trump has been chosen for this time of history; Trump is the 'Chosen One'; the Christian Nationalist movement makes up a large part of Trump's base

Trumpty says he's the 'Chosen One,'
A King, replete with a gold-plated crown.
Annointed by the 'religious right,'
They claim him as their guiding light.
Trumpty thrives on this adulation,
Bestowed adoringly by the Trump Nation.

Trumpty's much like Henry the Eight,*
A self-absorbed King of considerable weight.
He divorces the wives he no longer likes,
At least their heads aren't paraded on pikes.
He upends norms; he rules HIS way,
He overrides laws—in nary a day,
When some in his Court don't do as they're told,
They're banished to suffer a virtual scaffold.
He touts his manhood; he can't appear 'weak,'
He admires strong leaders (such as an Arab Sheik?)
Pity King Trumpty—his reign sad to see,
Akin to a Shakespearean tragedy.

*Henry the VIII of England (1509–1547)

Re: Article—(WAPO) Twelve signs Trump would try to run a fascist dictatorship in a second term (7/10/20); other news sources: Trump believes he is all-powerful, with free rein as President to do what he wants, defy laws See also Trumpty's MO, 'I Alone Can Fix It' and Health Hazards Ahead—Mental (un)Fitness, Delusional, Deranged

Trumpty thinks he's a Potentate,
A ruler divine of pre-ordained fate.
Sycophants hang on his every word,
Wearing red hats, they resemble a herd.
If they could, they'd camp on the White House lawn,
Crying MAGA* on cue from nighttime 'til dawn.
From his balcony window, Trump takes it all in,
'L'etat, c'est Trumpty'; Long live the King!

*Make America Great Again

Re: Articles—(WAPO) Trump paints a picture of a dystopian America that doesn't exist (2/11/17); (WAPO) Trump's delusions are about to blow up (7/9/18)

Trumpty acts like he's a King,
It's a dystopian kingdom he's living in.
When everything soon comes crashing down,
He'll find himself run out of town.
An oligarchy can't be sustained,
The end will come like a badly wrecked train.
Trump WILL be gone eventually,
Let's hope we still have a Democracy.

II

ALL THE PRESIDENT'S LIES!

The Lyin' King

Re: Article—(NYT) Why Trump supporters don't mind his lies (4/28/18); other news sources: CNN, Trump constantly lies; supporters don't care (4/3/19)

Trumpty Dumpty is in quite a stew,
So many lies! He knows NOT what to do.
He'll feed his supporters! His lies are their bread,
Whipped into a frenzy, they'll feast until bed.

(Apologies to 'Mother Goose')

Re: Article—(WAPO) How Trump can punish Iran without starting a war (9/18/19); other news sources: CNN, Trump says U.S. is "locked and loaded" to move into Iran See also The Great Divide, Foreign Policy Fiasco

Trumpty Dumpty, Deceiver-in-Chief,
Is wrecking our gov; that's his motif.
Can anyone trust he'll do as he says?
It's time to be rid of this lying Prez.
Congress, I plead—you must do your part,
To rein this guy in before any wars start!

Financial Failures

Re: Article—(WAPO) House sues Administration over Trump's tax returns (7/2/19); other news sources: CNN, NBC News, Trump fights subpoena of financial records (5/10/19)

Trumpty Dumpty is fit to be tied,
When his taxes reveal how much he has lied.
He'll sniff and he'll snarl and attack wildly,
Any and all who would dare disagree.
His goose is cooked and we might well surmise,
A jail term awaits; it'll be no surprise.

Re: Articles—(WAPO) Guide to the Supreme Court battle over Trump's tax returns and business records (5/12/20); (WAPO) Trump lawyers just made appalling arguments to the Supreme Court (5/12/20)

Trumpty Dumpty is fit to be tied,
When his finances show how much he has lied.
The family business is clearly suspect,
And Trumpty's on track for a major train wreck.
Will he survive? Who can foretell?
But Trumpty must know things cannot turn out well.

Re: Articles—(NYT) Deutsche Bank staff saw suspicious activity in Trump and Kushner* accounts (5/19/19); (WAPO) The fall of Deutsche Bank: Lies, greed, money laundering and Donald Trump (2/14/20)

*son-in-law Jared, and his father Charles Kushner

Trumpty Dumpty is caught-up in lies,
His finances show nefarious ties.
When family businesses almost tanked,
Bailouts came from a foreign bank.
U.S. lenders had turned him down,
And Eric and Don were sent out of town.
Deutsche-bag Bank came up with the dough,*
And saved the day—they're Russian, you know.
The Trump brand depends on offshore loans,
*The Regs** got it right! too many unknowns.*

*Deutsche Bank, an international financial institution (Germany), with a Russian subsidiary purportedly dealing in junk bonds
**U.S. banking regulators

Par for the Course
(Trumpty's golf)

Re: Article—(WAPO) U.S. taxpayers spent over $72 million on Trump golf outings (7/26/18); other news sources: Forbes, Trump golf trips could cost taxpayers over $340 million (7/10/19)

Obsessive Compulsive (Golf) Disorder

Trumpty spends his leisure time,
Golfing on the taxpayers' dime.
Mulligans—one or two—are allowed,
Ignore any protests from the crowd.
If he hits a ball into the rough,
No problem—just move it! if chipping's too tough.
He claims about twenty tournament wins,
At courses HE owns! Is that such a sin?
Golf's a great sport, but Trumpty's obsessed,
And never mind the Emoluments* mess.

*Emoluments clause of Constitution applicable to foreign influence—
a President cannot profit from foreign guests who pay to stay and play

Re: Article—(WAPO) A top Democrat warns:* If we don't confront Trump, he'll grow more lawless (a call for impeachment) (5/21/19)
*Rep. Jamie Raskin (D-MD)

Trumpty Dumpty is ripping US off,

A Commander-in-Cheat* that goes way beyond golf.

His fake TIME mag mugshot hangs on a wall,

In his prized Doral clubhouse—now that takes some gall!

With lawless gambling and broken morale,

He acts like the outlaws at O.K. Corral.**

*author Rick Reilly, *Commander-in-Cheat*
**livery and horse stable in Tombstone, AZ Territory; site of a famous shootout in the American Wild West

Re: Articles—(WAPO) Trump hired illegals to staff his Bedminster and Westminster golf courses (11/20/18); (WAPO) Trump's golf course employed undocumented workers (1/26/19); (WAPO) Trump Winery in Virginia fires illegals after grape harvest (12/31/19)

Hypocrite to the Core

Trumpty Dumpty made a bad call,
Trumpty Dumpty hired them all.
They came without papers but still they got in,
And were welcomed by Trumpty again and again.

Re: Articles—(WAPO) Trump has awarded next year's G-7 summit of world leaders to his Miami-area resort (10/17/19); (NYT) Trump will host next G-7 summit at his Doral resort (10/17/19); (WAPO) Trump pushes back on complaint of bed bugs at his Doral golf resort (8/27/19); other news sources: USA Today, Huffington Post, a guest reported 'voracious bed bugs' in room, lawsuit settled

Trumpty Dumpty is ripping US off,
The G-7 summit is all about golf.
The clubhouse features his fake TIME mag mug,
Trumpty approves! (he resembles a thug)
He claims rooms have "a magnificent view,"
Are those reserved for the privileged few?
And rumors of bed bugs—more infestation!
Congress, IMPEACH—for the sake of our nation!

III

FLY-BY-NIGHT ITINERARY
TRUMPTY'S TRAVELS

Saudi Arabia–May 21, 2017

Re: Article—(WAPO) Trump's bizarre and un-American visit to Saudi Arabia (5/21/17); on first foreign trip of Presidency, Trump meets with Crown Prince Salman and other royalty; after-dinner entertainment is a ceremonial sword dance; later at opening of the Global Center for Combating Extremist Ideology (GCCEI), all place hands on a glowing orb.

Will Trumpty wear a fancy fez,
On his first visit abroad as Prez?
He wants to impress Saudi Royalty,
By pledging our nation's loyalty.
Trumpty admires riches and power,
They praise effusively by the hour.
In the evening, a splendid sword dance
Is held in his honor; he joins in to prance.
The dancing and swaying goes into the night,
And Saudi's 'high-five'; 'this guy is all right!'

A Global Center to combat world terror,
Holds a grand opening while Trumpty is there.
A Celestial orb lights up the room,
With 'all hands-on' touching—does this erase gloom?
A symbolic gesture perhaps, for peace,
But that doesn't mean terror will cease.
Salman* and Trumpty are of the same breed,
Two troubled souls with a similar need.

*Crown Prince Mohammed bin Salman

France—July 14, 2017

Re: Article—(NYT) Trump and Macron cement unlikely friendship in Bastille Day visit (7/14/17); President and First Lady Melania have dinner in the Eiffel Tower with Emmanuel Macron and wife Brigitte; highlight of visit is military parade down the Champs-Elysees

Trumpty Drumpty does 'Francois,'
Of gay Par-ee—he is in awe!
He dines with Macron in the Eiffel Tower,
They talk and toast into a late hour.
They take in the view of Paris at night,
The city below—resplendent and bright.
On Bastille Day down the Champs-Elysee,
Armored tanks go on display.
An impressive parade put on by the host,
Large cheering crowds strike Trumpty the most.
He immediately plans a parade for US,
A competition for mightiness?

Large tanks and gunners; our bands will play,
With troops out in force on Veterans Day.
A grand Military—second to none,
Trumpty will say to the world, 'we won!'

Helsinki–July 16, 2018

Re: Article—(NYT) Trump, at Putin's side, questions U.S. intelligence on 2016 election (7/16/18)

Trumpty Dumpty wants bigly to see,
His old pal Vlad when in Helsinki.
They'll meet one-on-one, with no one else there,
No taping, no notes, no record to share.
With translators sworn to secrecy,
A blatant breech of diplomacy!
Trumpty and Putin later appear,
Each at a mike; from both—we soon hear.
"Did the Russians rig our last election?"
"Of course not," said Putin, dismissing the question.
"I believe Putin," Trump firmly retorts,
Rebuking all of our Intel reports.
Donnie and Vlad, a pair to see,
Their meeting will go down in history.

England–June 4, 2019

Re: Article—(WAPO) Trump's royal visit to the U.K...hosted by Queen Elizabeth II (6/4/19); President Trump brings along eight adult members of family—all attend a State banquet

Trumpty Dumpty visits the Queen,
With family in tow so all can be seen.
Publicity is what Trumpty craves most,
And the Queen will oblige as she is his host.
Outside, a Trump blimp bobs up and down,
Announcing to all that Trumpty's in town.
The First Lady plans to show off a Dior,
At the State dinner—do we care what she wore?
A grand tea is planned for the next afternoon,
Please spare US! This visit cannot end too soon.

South Korea–June 30, 2019

Re: Article—(NYT) Trump steps into North Korea and agrees with Kim Jong-un to resume talks (6/30/19); Trump is first U.S. President to enter N. Korea via the demilitarized zone (DMZ)

Trumpty Dumpty and best buddy Kim,
See the Nobel* as a prize they can win.
Kim freezes his nukes (except maybe a few),
In a deal that reeks of Pepe Le Pew.**
For a grand photo-op at the DMZ,
They shake hands and smile for the whole world to see.
Kim is playing Trumpty; he's done that before,
And Trumpty goes home empty-handed once more.

*Nobel Peace Prize
**Disney Looney Tunes character—a skunk

IV.

TRUMPTY'S MO
(MODUS OPERANDI)

'I Alone Can Fix It'

Trumpty Dumpty tests boundaries,
He does what HE wants; he doesn't say 'please.'
Our nation of laws is under attack,
By an Idiot-in-Chief who is fighting US back.
All 'rules be damned,' as he forges ahead,
He just doesn't care what Hamilton* said.
A fake Constitution exists in his mind,
Our arrogant Prez is appallingly blind.

*Alexander Hamilton, a framer of the U.S. Constitution, as was James Madison and other Founding Fathers

Re: Article—(WAPO) How the Trump administration weaponizes norms (5/27/20); other news sources: Historians: Trump upends norms of presidential behavior

Trumpty Dumpty goes full-out rogue,
Governing by fiat is now so in vogue.
He demands loyalty from all of his aides,
Do they not see how they are being played?

Congress, please ACT before it's too late,
*And take down this Prez—as in Watergate.**

*1972 political scandal that led to the resignation of President Richard Nixon

Re: Article—(WAPO) Who is to blame for the death of American Democracy—all of us! (9/23/19)

Trumpty Dumpty, Imposter-in-Chief,
Debases his office beyond belief.
He acts as he wants; he bends long-held rules,
What does he take US for—ignorant fools?
Who can contain him? But there'll come a day,
When smart voters act and put him away.
Trumpty will snarl and snivel and roar,
As he is being escorted out the front door.
Or more likely dragged out? Trumpty will fight!
*He WILL NOT go gentle in-to that good night.**

*Dylan Thomas

Re: Articles—(NYT) How Trump is using his power to pardon (6/1/18); (WAPO) Trump pardons Joe Arpaio, Maricopa County Sheriff, AZ (8/25/18); (NYT) Steve Brannon is arrested and charged with fraud in border wall campaign (8/20/20)

A Prediction?

Trumpty makes a terrible call,
When he decides to pardon them all.
*Bannon and Manafort, Gates, Stone, and Flynn,**
What a sad state our country is in.

And then there's Ivanka and Eric and Don,**
Do pardons extend to the kin of the Con?

*Trump allies Steve Bannon, Paul Manafort, Rick Gates, Roger Stone, Michael Flynn
**Adult children of the President

'I Take No Responsibility'
(Buck stops elsewhere!)

Re: Article—(WAPO) Donald Trump blames everyone else for his problems (5/8/17); other news sources: The Guardian, Trump says "no politician in history has been treated more unfairly than he has," alluding to the Press, in speech to graduates of the Coast Guard Academy (5/17/17)

Trumpty Dumpty blames everyone else,
But if truth be told, he should blame himself.
He calls the Press 'the enemy,'
Who have treated him terribly unfairly!
He blames 'fake news'; he blames CNN,
He'll blame Obama whenever he can.
He blames the Dems; he blames the Chinese,
Is there no end to this Trumpian sleaze?
The blame games reign—so childish, we know,
But blaming others is Trumpty's MO.

Re: Article—(WAPO) *Art of the Deal* author, Tony Schwartz: Why Trump can't change, no matter what the consequences (10/18/19); Trump views the world as a 'dark, dangerous place teeming with enemies out to get him'

Trumpty Dumpty goes after the Press,
Whom he'll attack is anyone's guess!
He calls out a reporter speaking the truth,
"It's fake news," he says, 'Where is your proof?'
He just can't admit he may be at fault,
He'll blame someone else when he gets caught.
It's the Art of the Deal—pure projection,
He still can't get over his own election.

Exact Revenge!
(Attack-dog)

Re: Article—(WAPO) Comey firing: reactions from members of Congress on FBI director's sudden dismissal (5/9/17); James Comey was leading an investigation into Russian interference in 2016 election; in an earlier one-on-one closed-door meeting, Comey would not pledge his 'loyalty,' angering Trump

Trumpty goes after the FBI,
And fires Jim Comey, on the fly?
Comey "was crazy, a real nut job,"
'Lordy,' says Comey; 'did I just get robbed?'

Comey would not pledge his loyalty,
The guy had to go! Can we not see?
Can Trump brush this off? (he always escapes)
"Lordy!" says Comey, "I hope there are tapes."
Revenge is a part of Trumpty's MO,
Trumpty's the 'nut job'; that we all know.

Re: Articles—(WAPO) Trump's mean streak spares no one—living or dead (12/21/19); at post-impeachment rally in Battle Creek, MI, Trump suggests the late Congressman John Dingell is 'burning in hell' over wife's vote to impeach; (WAPO) Rep. Debbie Dingell (D-MI) thanks colleagues for their support...(2/19/20) See also Impeachment Travails, Acquittal Travesty

Trumpty, our Attack-Dog-in-Chief,
Chews up Democracy—this dog is a thief!
He tears our Constitution to shreds,
He doesn't read—he'd care not what it said.
When someone angers him, Trumpty bites back.
To get his revenge, this dog will attack!
Is nothing sacred? Not in his head,
No one is spared; not even the dead.
He invokes the memory of Congressman Dingell,*
Who's "maybe looking up" (from hell?)
Instead of down—from Heaven's gate?
Please muzzle this beast; it's dangerous to wait!

*Former Congressman John Dingell (D-MI)

Re: Article—(WAPO) Trump takes on Judge Amy Berman Jackson ahead of Roger Stone sentencing (2/12/20); other news sources: sentence guideline recommended by prosecutors—7–9 years

Trumpty Dumpty goes after a Judge,*
Trumpty never holds back a grudge.
He denigrates Jackson's sworn right to rule,
On Roger Stone's** jail time—so 'unjust and cruel!'
SHE has the right to decide this man's fate?
His unfounded rants boil over with hate.

*U.S. District Judge, Amy Berman Jackson
**long-time Trump ally and advisor

Confront, Defend

Re: Article—(WAPO) Trump's 'jokes' are totally killing me (9/18/17); other news sources: CNN, Jake Tapper interview with White House staffer re: Trump's off-the-cuff comments on Covid-19 testing (6/21/20); interview script also on CNN.com

Trumpty Is our National joke!
Entertainer-in-Chief and laughing-stock bloke.
When we hear controversial words from our Prez,
"He was making a joke," the White House staff says.
Impulsive ad-libbing—hard to walk back,
Defend, if you can when under attack.
His comments on testing are truly sad,
"By doing all this testing, it makes us look bad."
It's a "tongue-in-cheek" comment, the staffer said,
A lame excuse—WE know what we read.

Re: Article—(WAPO), Trump's ridiculous defense of his comments about injecting disinfectants to ward off Coronavirus—White House press conference (4/24/20) See also Virus Crisis!

A defensive Trumpty walks it back,
He's done that before when he's under attack.
"I was being sarcastic!" he will say,
When reporters start having a field day.
If criticized, he can't let it go,
"It's not what I said"; it's his MO.

Distract, Divert
(Wag-the-dog)

Trumpty excels at 'wagging the dog,'
And leads US into an endless fog,
Clueless, like the slow-boiling frog,
He croaks away to an ad-miring bog.

(Apologies to Emily Dickinson)

Re: Articles—(WAPO) Trump orders attack on Iran (1/3/20); (WAPO) Trump's order to kill Soleimani* is ready to backfire (1/7/20); Trump accused of a 'wag-the-dog' strike to distract from Senate impeachment trial
*Iranian commander, Gen. Qassem Soleimani

Trumpty's devious to the core,
'Wag-the-dog' and start a war.
Distract from impeachment was his plan,
He's nothing but a conniving con man.

Re: Article—(NYT) Andrew McCabe, ex-FBI official, will not be charged (2/14/20); his indictment had been sought following Trump accusation of FBI corruption; other news sources: Yahoo news, 'house of cards' built by Trump in effort to discredit the FBI and distract from his mounting problems is collapsing (2/14/20); McCabe news is latest structural blow to a crumbling edifice

Trumpty, our nation's sociopath,
Spews forth accusatorial wrath.
Andrew McCabe may be off the hook,
But will others* be given a second look?
No one has been criminally charged,
Close to collapsing is Trump's 'house of cards.'

*FBI/Intel officials—James Comey, Peter Strzok, Lisa Page, John Brennan, Rep. Adam Schiff (D-CA) Bruce Ohr (and others), investigating whether Trump campaign conspired with Russia on election interference

V.

'YOU'RE TERRIBLE PEOPLE'

Immigration Mess
(Fear, paranoia of the 'other')

News, several sources: Early in Presidency, Trump issues Executive Order banning entrance of foreign nationals from seven Muslin countries into U.S. (90-day ban) (1/27/17); blocked Syrian refugees indefinitely from entering the U.S.—a testing of the Constitution (1/28/17)

Trumpty signs a travel ban,
For reasons unclear; because he can?
It stops mainly Muslims from entering our space,
Is this because they're a different race?
To Bannon and Miller,* the signing is Yuuge,
They high-five each other; Trumpty's their stooge.
During his campaign he went after a judge.**
Likewise, the Kahn's*** because of a grudge.
Immigration's in flux as never before!
The welcome mat pulled; it's not there anymore.

*Steve Bannon and Stephen Miller, White House aides
**Judge Gonzalo P. Curiel, U.S. District Court, San Diego, presiding over class action case against Trump University
***Khizr and Ghazala Kahn, a 'Gold Star' family whose son, Captain Kahn, was killed in Iraq war and named an American Hero

Re: Article—(WAPO) Children crying at U.S. border and sitting in cages (6/20/18); other news sources: CNN, the inhumane treatment of children detained at the border; packed into cages for indefinite time

Trumpty Dumpty hasn't a clue,
He's like the 'Old Woman Who Lived in a Shoe.'
With so many children who need to be fed,
He'll whip them all soundly and put them to bed
On a cold concrete floor with no blankets in sight,
They'll cry and they'll shiver throughout the long night.
Such inhumane treatment puts US to shame!
Trumpty will claim the Dems are to blame.

(Apologies to 'Mother Goose')

Re: Article—(WAPO) The core of Donald Trump's immigration policy? Fear (8/24/17)

> *Trumpty Dumpty's failed the test,*
> *Of what it would take for him to 'Be Best.'*
> *He sees immigrants as unworthy beings,*
> *Unless they have with them significant means.*
> *People with money are welcome to stay,*
> *While poor folk who enter will be sent away.*

Re: Article—(WAPO) Trump's far-fetched proposal on immigration control at the southwestern border (10/4/19); building a border wall surrounded by a moat

> *Trumpty Dumpty takes a great fall,*
> *Into the moat surrounding his wall.*
> *Venomous snakes and crocs/crooks attack,*
> *He's knee-deep in muck; how will he fight back?*
> *Trumpty is desperate—he just wants a win,*
> *But this cockeyed proposal? It will do him in.*

Census Consensus
(Illegals don't count)

News, several sources: Supreme Court puts hold on Administration's effort to add a citizenship question to the 2020 census (Court took into consideration MALDEF* advocacy in an Alabama decision) (6/27/19)

*Mexican American Legal Defense and Educational Fund

Background: With inclusion of question on citizenship, illegals may not respond to a census survey and would be left out of total population count (ultimately affecting Congressional House seats, determined by number of people living in a State)

Re: Article—(NYT) Justice Dept. reverses course on citizenship question on census, citing Trump's orders (7/3/19); other news sources: Justice Dept will press its search for legal grounds to force inclusion of a citizenship question on 2020 Census (7/5/19)

Trumpty Dumpty defies a Court ruling,
On the Citizen question—but who is he fooling?
Trumpty has always gotten his way,
And cannot accept that the Court has its say.
So he puts forth new orders to do as he says,
People, wake up! And vote out this Prez!

Re: Article—(WAPO) Trump administration changes its story on the census citizenship question (7/11/19)

Trumpty Dumpty is at it again,
By defying a Court ruling he gets a big WIN.
His latest demands on the Citizen question,
Are causing confusion—is that his intention?
"Executive orders do not override"*
Supreme Court decisions—THEY are our guide.

*Thomas A. Saenz, General Counsel in Maryland, and Counsel for MALDEF

Update (9/10/20): Federal court in New York blocks Trump order to exclude undocumented immigrants from census count

---

Just Go Away!
(Trumpty's prejudices)

Re: Article—(WAPO) Trump's incoherent monologue on homelessness in America (7/2/19)

Trumpty Dumpty, Bigot-in-Chief,
Spews hatred of 'others,' sowing much grief!
He views the homeless as worthless strays,
Who roam through our streets and alleyways.
'They disgrace our cities'; our workers* won't stay,
To Trumpty, the homeless should just go away!

*downtown professionals (also visitors)

Re: Article—(NYT) Trump tells Congresswomen to 'go back' to the countries they came from (7/14/19); Fox News, Trump sicced rally crowd on The Squad,* Greenville, NC (7/17/19)

Trumpty Dumpty, our racist Prez,
Lashes forth with his grievances.
He wants members of Congress—four 'second-class' beings,*
To go back to their countries; whatever that means!
They're 'shrill and disruptive' in wanting their say,
To Trumpty, they all need to just go away!

*Reps. Alexandria Ocasio-Cortez (D-NY); Ilhan Omar (D-MN)
Ayanna Pressley, (D-MA); Rashida Tlaib, (D-MI)

Racism Run Rampant
(Racial injustice)

Trumpty promotes racial fights,
Making a sham of our Civil Rights.
He'll pit a person against his own brother,
Particularly when it's people of color.
Where is humanity and common sense?
Hatred surrounds US—are we all dense?

Re: Article—(NYT) A guide to the Charlottesville aftermath (8/13/17); other news sources: CNN, White Nationalist rally: What we know (8/13/17); (WAPO) The 'very fine people' at Charlottesville —Who were they? (5/8/20)

Trumpty blew it in Charlottesville,
His words that day did not go well.
With "very fine people on both sides,"
Trump began a dangerous slide.
With his true feelings on blatant display,
Voters WILL surely rue the day.

Re: Article—(NYT) 8 minutes and 46 seconds: How George Floyd was killed in police custody (5/31/20); other news sources, video, CNN, With a shocking invocation of George Floyd, Trump shows his disconnect from nation's pain (6/6/20); brags about a strong economy; Joe Biden calls Trump's remarks 'despicable'

We remember George Floyd at his last breath,
On national TV—a most horrible death.
Watching it 'live' should make US all seethe,
As he gasps and cries out, "I can't breathe!"
Sadly, the term, 'taking a knee,'
Morphed into lethal reality.
From the President of our nation,
There came no words of consolation.
Trump brushed it off; so callous is he,
He just doesn't care—no empathy.
"George is looking down right now,"
A heartless remark we must disavow!
"It's a great thing that is happening
For our country"...a "great day for him."*
Trump's disconnected, deranged 'insight'?
The man is despicable! Biden is right.

*At press conference, Trump cites a booming economy in an incoherent rant

Re: Article—(WAPO) LaFayette Square clash, still reverberating, becomes an iconic episode of Donald Trump's presidency (6/13/20)

Trumpty is our Racist-in-Chief,
Causing our country untold grief!
Protesters gathered; peaceful were they,
But soon to be tear-gassed by end of the day.
He walked to the Square; surely a 'win,'
Surrounded by toadies within his Admin.
Holding a Bible (that he never reads),
A 'prop' photo-op, while our nation grieves.
Chants from the street of 'Black Lives Matter!'
Are ignored by Trumpty as empty chatter.
This confrontation in LaFayette Square,
Will be his downfall; we were ALL there.

VI

THE GREAT DIVIDE

Domestic Dissention
(Law and dis-order)

Re: Article—(WAPO) Trump frames El Paso shooting as his side against his opponents (8/6/19); other news sources: ABC, NPR, Trump administration embraces white nationalism; shooter was a White Supremist

Trumpty Dumpty, Divider-in-Chief,
Loves to spew hatred (I'll try to be brief)!
He says we are "doing incredibly well,"
But under this Prez, it feels like h*ll.
Why do we put up with a raging buffoon?
Removal of Trumpty can't happen too soon.

Re: Article—(WAPO) House Democrats tell Mitch McConnell to pass stricter gun laws (8/7/19); other news sources: NPR, 145 CEOs call on Senate to pass 'common-sense, bipartisan' gun laws (9/12/19)

Trumpty Dumpty gets fearful and runs,
When the NRA brings out its big guns.
Trumpty won't dare confront LaPierre,*
2020 is looming; his support must be there.

Trumpty sees guns as a way he can win,
And so he keeps playing US again and again.
Moscow Mitch** is in on the plan,
To delay gun control as long as they can.

*Wayne LaPierre, CEO, National Rifle Association
**Senate Majority Leader, Mitch McConnell (R-KY)

Re: Articles—(NYT) As Trump pushes into Portland (Ore.), his campaign ads turn darker (7/22/20); (WAPO) Portland's mayor tear-gassed by Federal agents amid a tense meeting with protesters (7/23/20); other news sources: CNN, NBC, Trump campaign promotes dark and exaggerated portrayal of Democrat-led cities; (WAPO) Trump's 'Operation Legend' was supposed to combat crime...is new political stunt (7/24/20)

Trumpty orders in the Feds,
Tearing our Constitution* to shreds.
Secret police in unmarked cars
Patrol clandestinely after-hours.
Local enforcement is given the boot,
While Federal troops have power to shoot.
Peaceful protesters want their say,
As they are tear-gassed (they're in the way)!
A Dem-ruled city of 'lawless beings,'
Trump says, "It's worse than anyone's seen."
A dictator Prez directs from afar.
With help from his AG, William Barr.
And a role for Homeland Security,**
A 'win' for Trumpty politically?

But it's far from finished; next it may be,
Chicago, IL or Albuquerque.
Trumpty's Op Legend means Federal control,
Law and dis-order; he's on a roll.
A legacy of this Presidency:
The most corrupt in history.

*1st Amendment, a right to peaceful assembly; 4th Amendment, prohibits unreasonable search and seizure
**Custom and border patrol agents deployed to cities

Foreign Policy Fiasco

Re: Articles—(NYT) Trump throws Middle East policy into turmoil over Syria (10/7/19); (WAPO) Republicans assail Trump's decision to pull troops from northern Syria (10/8/19); other news sources: CNN, Trump's betrayal of the Kurds is a gift to Putin and Assad…'major blunder' (10/8/19)

Trumpty double-crosses again,
Impulsively acting—so ISIS* can win?
He tosses diplomacy right on its head,
Supporters will cheer, "he's doing what he said!"
He gave Erdogan** a glowing green light,
To crush our Kurdish allies on sight.
Why would he do that? Was it his plan?
Trumpty will say—'because I can.'

On orders from Putin? That is not known,
But it's likely he didn't act all alone.

*Islamic State of Iraq and Syria
**President Recep Tayyip Erdogan, Turkey

Re: Article—(NYT) Trump followed his gut on Syria, calamity came fast (10/14/20); other news sources: Turkey, Syria, Russia benefit from Trump's impulsiveness (10/8/19)

Trumpty Dumpty, Putin's slave,
Is digging himself an early grave.
His betrayal of allies is over the top,
Will no one confront him? He just cannot stop.
Is he working for US—or some foreign state?
We all need to know before it's too late!

Re: Article—(NYT) Pulling of U.S. troops from Syria could aid Assad and ISIS (10/7/19); other news sources: CNN, Syria-Turkey crisis: Putin now owns this mess (10/20/19); ISIS is free to run and regroup

Trumpty Dumpty abandons the Kurds,
How cruel is that? There aren't any words.
How DO we control him? It's doubtful we will,
Now ISIS is free to pursue their roadkill.
As Putin toasts this fortuitous WIN,
Syria and Turkey are joining right in.
It's BLOOD ON Trump's HANDS for the whole world to see,
A foreign fiasco—Trump's legacy.

Re: Article—(NYT) Pullback leaves Green Berets feeling 'ashamed' and Kurdish allies describing 'betrayal' (10/13/19); other news sources: NBC, Putin, Assad and Turkey celebrate (10/15/19)

A tale of terror: Headless Horseman Trumpty

Mad King Trumpty loses his head,
And chaos and terror reign in his stead.
Havoc takes over the global stage,
As our headless Trumpty rides forth in a rage.
It's time to be rid of this Halloween horror,
Voters, unite! Show him the door!

Re: Articles—(NYT) Abu Bakr al-Baghdadi, ISIS leader known for his brutality is dead (10/27/19); (WAPO) Trump's announcement of al-Baghdadi's death…marked by bravado, misleading boasts and taunts (10/28/19); U.S. raid on commando base in NW Syria

Trumpty picks a global fight,
(mis)Using military might.
"This really bad guy had to go!"
An ISIS Commander; that's what we know.
Our 'copters strike a Syrian base,
Leading to International disgrace.
Was this attack done on a whim?
That's what we've come to expect of him.
'I was the one who took Baghdadi down!'
'I didn't get credit, Waaa, Waaa,' cries our clown.

Re: Articles—(WAPO) Trump has raised strategic incoherence to new levels with Soleimani's* killing (1/3/20); (WAPO) Trump's purported motive—to distract from upcoming impeachment trial (1/3/20) See also Trumpty's MO, Distract, Divert, and Impeachment Travails, Acquittal Travesty

Trumpty Dumpty orders drone strikes,
On an enemy leader whom no one likes.
He takes out a General* in Iran,
To distract from impeachment? That was his plan.

*Gen. Qassem Soleimani, Iran's top commander

VII.

THE REVOLVING DOOR

Re: Article—(NYT) Turnover at the top of the Trump administration (3/16/18); other news sources: Trump's staff leave White House in unprecedented numbers (wide-ranging time period, beginning early in Trump presidency); by 2020, 60+ people forced out or resigned

Trumpty Dumpty purges his staff,
They work for a while, then are given the shaft.
He claims he will hire the 'very best' folk,
But keeping them on has become quite a joke.
*Exit Tillerson, Nielsen, Price, Flynn and Haley,**
Others to follow—just watch this space daily.
*Now it's Acosta;** no doubt they'll be more,*
Trump's legacy is: a revolving door!

*Administration officials: Rex Tillerson, Kristin Nielsen, Tom Price, Michael Flynn, Nikki Haley
**Alexander Acosta, Secretary of Labor, resigned 7/12/19

Repeated postings

Now it's Dan Coats;* no doubt they'll be more,...etc.

*Dan Coats, Director of National Intelligence, resigned 7/28/19
Now it's John Bolton, National Security Advisor, resigned 9/10/19
Now It's Rick Perry, Secretary of Energy, resigned 10/17/19

Re: Articles—(WAPO) John Bolton out as National Security Advisor after clashing with Trump (9/10/19); (WAPO) Why Bolton didn't testify in the impeachment inquiry (6/22/20); other news sources: USA Today, "Let's be clear; I resigned." John Bolton contradicts Donald Trump on whether he was fired; Trump's ranting comments about Bolton (7/17/20)

Another one bites the dust,
Bolton lost Trumpty's trust.
He played both sides, don't you see,
Loyal to Trump—to a degree.
Part of a team, but then he turned,
And Trumpty soon began a slow burn.
Bolton questioned Trump's role in Ukraine,
And quickly found himself off the Trump train.
The Dems hoped Bolton would help them out,*
For he could bring some major clout.
"It will all come out—in my book,"
He's off a testimonial hook?
Trumpty called Bolton a "lowlife dummy,"
But Trump is the lowlife! The comment was crummy.
Nonsensical politics on full display,
Will it be Bolton who has the last say?

*by testifying in House impeachment inquiry

Re: Article—(NYT) Trump to fire Intelligence watchdog who had key role in Pandemic Response Accountability (4/3/20); other news sources: Real Clear Politics, 'Deep State' firing of several Inspectors General in 'one fell swoop'; some IGs were from Obama administration. (5/1-17/20)

Trumpty Dumpty fires IGs,*
All were 'against him'; he was NOT pleased!
Some were held over from Obama's reign,
Some were never on the Trump train.
A revengeful Trumpty firing binge?
Our Prez is sadly becoming unhinged!

*Michael Atkinson, Intel Community IG

Glenn Fine, Defense Dept IG, Acting; Pandemic Response Accountability

Christi Grimm, Health and Human Services IG, Acting

Steve Linick, State Dept IG

Mitch Behm, Transportation Dept IG, Acting

Also fired, Joseph McGuire, Acting Dir. of National Intelligence (investigating Russian meddling in upcoming 2020 election)

Re: Articles—(NYT) U.S. attorney in Manhattan* said he would step down, ending standoff with Justice Dept (6/20/20); (WAPO) Trump ousts Manhattan U.S. attorney who investigated president's associates (6/21/20); Berman agrees to leave after assurances a trusted deputy would replace him

*Geoffrey S. Berman, U.S. Attorney for Southern District of New York

Trump and his toady, Billy Barr,*
Are kindred souls; what bullies they are!
Berman went after Trump's pal Rudy,**

On financial shenanigans—it was his duty.
Trump wasn't happy! This guy had to go,
So, 'Geoffrey, you're fired.' (like on his old show)***
Berman resisted—strongly, we heard,
"I will not resign," but Trump had the last word.
Billy and Trumpty—comrades, for sure,
Their revolting charade leaves a foul o-dor.

*Attorney General William Barr
**Rudy Guiliani, Trump's personal attorney
***The Apprentice

VIII

THE GREAT (NON)COMMUNICATOR

Twitter Trumpty

Several news sources: The New Yorker.com, How Trump governs by tweet: start with outrage, then escalate (10/11/17); Trump spends morning hurling all-caps tweets while COVID-19 spirals out of control (7/9/20)

> *Trumpty Dumpty governs by tweet,*
> *He tweets and tweets; then stops to eat.*
> *With burgers and fries to fortify him,*
> *He goes on tweeting ad nauseum.*
> *No one can stop him, although some have tried,*
> *Aides won't confront him; they're petrified.*
> *'It's my right to tweet! I'm boss of you.'*
> *'So lay off,' says Trumpty, 'It's just what I do!'*

Re: Article—(WAPO) Doctored images have become a fact of life for political campaigns (1/14/20); other news sources: CBS, Images of Senate Minority Leader Schumer (D-NY) and Speaker Pelosi (D-CA) in Arab attire—turban and hijab, retweeted by Trump (1/14/20); tweet falsely claims 'the two most powerful Democrats in Congress have come to the Ayatollah's rescue'

Trumpty's tweets are out of control,
He's become our resident White House troll.
He puts out photos of fake Arab attire,
On Pelosi and Schumer—his targets of ire.
Voters, awake! I'm counting on you,
To turn our country a bright shade of blue.

Teleprompter Trumpty

Re: Article—(WAPO) Teleprompter Trump meets Twitter Trump as the president responds to mass slayings (8/5/19); delivers prepared speech from teleprompter on scourge of 'destructive partisanship,' that was preceded by free-style tweeting attacking 'fake news,' and immigration

Teleprompt Trumpty reads haltingly,
The words have no meaning in his delivery.
He tries to convince US all will be fine,
But saying 'we're united' is plain flat-out lying.
By contrast, his tweets decry an INVASION,
Of people who want to take over our nation.
The Twitter accounts expose Trumpty's core,
I'm ashamed for our country and can't take much more!

Cellular Trumpty

Re: Article—(WAPO) Phone logs in impeachment report renew concern about security of Trump communications (12/6/19); other news sources: CNN, Trump still uses personal phone despite warnings (12/6/19); Trump makes calls from White House on personal phone using unsecured lines—anyone can listen

Trumpty Dumpty loves his cell phone,
That he uses for calls to people unknown.
Security? Trumpty's oblivious to rules,
Russians can listen; hackers have tools.
Did hackers go after his old pal Rudy?*
For Trumpty, security's not a prime duty.
He gets by with this! Are we numb to it all?
It's Trumpty EXPOSED, as he makes a call.

*Rudy Giuliani,
Trump's personal attorney

The (mis)Spoken Word

Re: Article—(WAPO) U.S. consumers, not China, pay for tariffs on imports (5/12/19); other news sources: Newsmax, Reuters, Trump warns China (by tweet) not to retaliate on tariffs—would hurt U.S. consumers (5/13/19)

Trumpty loves illiterate folk,
And it's clear that he does; that is no joke.
For HE's one of them as his bad tweeting shows,
Full of misspellings and challenging prose.
It's "by" for 'buy' and "their" for 'there,'
Also, "non-tariffed"? Does Trumpty not care?
He says Joe Biden has 'lost a step,'
But Trumpty's the one who seems most inept.
He has "oranges" for 'origins' in Mueller's probe,
And new names for leaders around the globe.
The Israeli P.M. is "Betanyahu,"
Trumpty's rendition of Netanyahu?*
It's what we expect from this moronic Prez,
We're forced to examine each word that he says.

*Prime Minister Benjamin Netanyahu, Israel

Re: Article—(WAPO) Trump appears to slur his speech during remarks…U.S. would recognize Jerusalem as Israel's capital (12/8/19); other news sources: ABC, CBS, Trump slurs, mis-uses words during speech at Hershey, PA rally (12/10/19) See also Health Hazards Ahead—Mental (un)Fitness, Ignorant, Illiterate

Trumpty Dumpty slurs his words,
His malaprop speaking is one for the birds!
United 'Shtates,' and also 'Jeruz,'*
Mangled words do not amuse.
He conflates Tim Cook of Apple renown,
And calls him 'Tim Apple'—par for this clown.
Remember the '2 Corinthians'?
Biblical knowledge is pure pretense.
And 'sock rocket' (stock market)? Give me a break,
Trumpty's incompetence just takes the cake!

*Jerusalem

Re: Article—(WAPO) What Trump was talking about in his baffling rant about wind energy (12/23/19); rambles on about fumes and birds being killed by turbines, which he calls 'windmills'

Donnie Quixote* dreams bigly for sure,
He chases fake fumes and windmills that whirr…
"You know, I know windmills very much,"
Huh? Incoherence in a clutch?
He goes on to say turbines cause cancer,
He's thought about cancer and has the answer.

His wind 'expertise' is one for the birds,
As he rides forth to battle with fool-hardy words.

*fictional Nobleman Don Quixote de la Mancha

Forecaster-in-Chief (Sharpie-gate)

Re: Article—(WAPO) 'We worked for NOAA'—weather forecasting should not be political (9/4/19); Trump shows how Hurricane Dorian is forecast to 'hit or graze' Alabama

Trumpty Dumpty, Forecaster-in-Chief,
Wrecks his havoc and brings US much grief.
He bends NOAA's rules with a stroke of his Sharpie,
How long must we put up with all this malarkey?
Voters—unite! and show him the door,
Quoth The Raven, "Nevermore."*

*Edgar Allan Poe

Re: Article—(WAPO) Trump shows a doctored hurricane chart (9/5/19); other news sources: Washington Examiner, Trump doubles down on insistence his Alabama forecasting tweet was correct; shows altered graphic in Oval Office—an outdated forecasting model; Trump tweet: to destroy a hurricane, 'bomb the eye' (8/26/19)

Trumpty Dumpty, Forecaster-in-Chief,
Is testing NOAA beyond belief!
The hurricane cone is whatever HE says,
And includes Alabama. 'So there!' says our Prez.
He says we can "nuke the hurricane eye."
Is Trumpty serious? It's a long-debunked lie.
He lives in his own reality,
On public display for the world to see.

IX

MUELLER 'HOAX'

Special Counsel Robert Mueller's investigation of 2016 election

Re: Articles—(NYT) Mueller will release a damaging report that details Russian interference in 2016 election (3/18/19); (WAPO) Mueller to testify before Congress (7/24/19)

Trumpty Dumpty sits high on his wall,
And casts down upon US a terrible pall.
He blames Mueller time and that thing he calls 'Russier,'
Such was The Fall of the (Great) House of Usher.*
Our nation's in peril; will this be our fate?
Can we recognize danger before it's too late?
We'll hear now from Mueller, whose truth will prevail,
Will the endgame for Trumpty be time served in jail?

*Edgar Allan Poe

Robert Mueller's testimony before Congress (7/24/19):

Counselor Mueller looked tired and sad,
And his verbal performance was shockingly bad.

His well-earned credentials were not on display,
With curtailed answers defining the day.
We should have expected he'd go by the book,
But hoped he would give US a personal look
Into obstruction by our corrupt Prez,
He stoically stood by what his report says.

Re: Articles—(NYT) Judge calls Barr's handling of Mueller Report 'distorted' and 'misleading' (3/7/19); other news sources: Newsweek, Attorney General William Barr is loyal to Trump, not U.S. says NYC Bar Association; (NYT) Barr seized on Epstein case as doubts mounted about Justice Dept. (10/23/19); Barr purportedly visited Jeffery Epstein,* being held in Federal custody, around time of Epstein's suicide

*American financier and sex offender arrested July 6, 2019, accused of abuse of young girls; died in Federal custody by suicide Aug. 10, 2019

Trumpty Dumpty must love William Barr,
The best FIXER-upper for Trumpty by far.
For the Mueller Report, coded redactions,
Covered for Trumpty's nefarious actions.
Allegations of spying? What more, pray-thee-tell?
Trumpty must know things cannot turn out well.
And then there is Epstein; what does Barr know?
So many questions—and miles to go.

Re: Article—(WAPO) Barr faces fresh scrutiny over Roger Stone sentencing, after four prosecutors resign from DOJ following Barr's interference (2/12/20); Barr had changed recommended sentence after a Trump tantrum

Trumpty Dumpty defends Barr again,
When Barr recommends less time in the pen
For friend Roger Stone, 'a really good guy,'
Barr is Trump's toady—we cannot deny.

Re: Article—(NYT) Impeachment investigators exploring whether Trump lied to Mueller…in written answers provided in the Russia investigation (11/18/19)

Trumpty Dumpty is fit to be tied,
When new evidence shows how much he has lied.
Grand jury records confirm our suspicion,
That Trumpty is going down the road to perdition.

Re: Article—(WAPO) Trump asserts Executive privilege over Mueller Report (5/8/19); other news sources: Politico, The Guardian, Justice Department tries to block testimony on how Trump tried to end Russia investigation, as detailed in Mueller's report (12/11/19)

Trumpty Dumpty has hatched a bold plan,
To stonewall and block all that he can.
Ms Hicks'* testimony turned into a sham,
Will that be the case with Counsel McGahn?**
He counts on the Courts to be his best friend,
Lawsuits go on—and on—'til they end.
Like Zootopia*** sloths, he'll act in slow-motion,
And outlast the Dems who have not a notion.
Put off 'til tomorrow any task for today,
For Trumpty, a new term depends on delay.

*Hope Hicks, former Trump aide and Communications Director, refusing to answer questions in House impeachment inquiry
**White House Counsel Don McGahn
***Zootopia—2016 movie, Disney Animation Studios

IMPEACHMENT TRAVAILS

Pre-impeachment Scuttle

Re: Articles—(NYT) Trump has disqualified himself from running in 2020 (10/1/19); (NYT) Trump rails against 'flimsy' articles of impeachment by 'radical' Democrats (12/10/19)

> *Trumpty Dumpty distorts the truth,*
> *Confronted with facts, he'll say, 'there's no proof.'*
> *His command of 'what's true' is a self-serving key,*
> *To remain in the White House; do we not see?*
> *Impeachment won't happen—"a hoax," Trumpty says,*
> *Congress—stand up! Get rid of this Prez.*

Re: Article—(WAPO) We investigated the Watergate* scandal. We believe Trump should be impeached (signed by 17 former prosecutors) (10/17/19) See also All the President's Lies!

*1972 political scandal that led to resignation of President Richard Nixon

> *As Trumpty Dumpty tweets out his lies,*
> *He self-destructs in front of our eyes.*
> *Can we not see what's happening here?*
> *But lucky for US there is a cure.*

Congress can act before it's too late,
And take down this Prez—as in Watergate!

Re: Articles—(WAPO) Trump's presidency was rotten from the start—it's time to cleanse the White House (10/10/19); (WAPO) Why Trump can't stop all witnesses from testifying in impeachment inquiry (10/15/19); (WAPO) More than 500 law professors say Trump committed 'impeachable conduct' (12/6/19)

Trumpty Dumpty has hit a new low,
With hate-filled attacks, primarily for show.
At rallies, his insults are over the top,
Will no one contain him? He just cannot stop.
Congress, it's time to SHOW HIM THE DOOR,
Impeach and convict! Do it soon—I implore.

Re: Article—(WAPO) Ann Telnaes cartoon showing Trump with long necktie, ready to lynch (10/23/19); caption: The only 'lynching' Trump is experiencing…is the one he is doing to himself with his unethical and impeachable actions

Trumpty Dumpty says there's a lynching,
The thought of Jim Crow leaves most of US flinching.
Has Trumpty forgotten our history?
He flings his words so recklessly.
Trumpty's a master at stirring up hate,
*IMPEACH this Prez now—as in Watergate!**

*President Nixon resigned before a Congressional vote on recommendation to impeach

Re: Article—(WAPO) Trump's ex-Russia adviser Fiona Hill told impeachment investigators of Giuliani's* efforts in Ukraine (10/15/19); other news sources: The Guardian, Impeachment inquiry: Sondland's** bombshell testimony blows holes in Trump's Ukraine defense (11/20/19)

*Rudy Giuliani, Trump's personal attorney
**Gordon Sondland, U.S. Ambassador to European Union, 2018-2020; fired by Trump

> *Trumpty Dumpty rules like a King,*
> *It's a shadow gov he operates in.*
> *He staffed it with swampy crocs/crooks and creeps,*
> *S. Miller* no doubt will stay on for keeps.*
> *It's past time for US to take back what is ours,*
> *Congress, please ACT—we gave you those powers!*

*White House aide Stephen Miller

Re: Article—(WAPO) U.S. vs Lev Parnas et al. Indictment… in Manhattan federal court (10/17/19); other news sources: USA Today, NBC, Guiliani associates Lev Parnas and Igor Fruman in Trump-Ukraine controversy arrested on campaign finance charges (10/20/19); See also The Revolving Door—firing of U.S. District attorney, Geoffrey S. Berman

> *Trumpty Dumpty, Mafia Don,*
> *Is starring in 'The Art of the Con.'*
> *He gets Guiliani to do his bidding,*
> *They are up to no-good; who are they kidding?*
> *Guili taps Russians Parnas and Fruman,*
> *Two most unsavory species of vermin.*

*They'll offer Ukraine a Quid Pro Quo,**
That'll stay under cover; no one will know,
Unless someone sings! How bad would that look?
Deny and deny! says the Mobster playbook.

*something given in exchange for something else (a favor)

Acquittal Travesty

Re: Article—(WAPO) Trump diatribe on Impeachment as an 'attempted coup,' eve of House impeachment inquiry (12/17/19)

A raging Trumpty belittles US all,
As he slowly begins to fall from his wall.
'An attempted coup,' he defiantly says,
He'll never accept removal as Prez.

Re: Article—(WAPO) Trump embraces rally…supporters listen and cheer (12/19/19); holds post-impeachment rally in Battle Creek, MI See also Trumpty's MO, Exact Revenge!

Trumpty cries he's 'under assault,'
"I did nothing wrong"; it's all the Dems fault.
'The witches and Jesus fared better than I,'*
'They got due process'—his angry reply!
He went on to say, "I committed no crime,"
In fact, "I'm having a (very) good time."

*Salem Witch Trials (1692)

Re: Article—(WAPO) Trump blames House Speaker Nancy Pelosi, whose "teeth were falling out of her mouth and she didn't have time to think" (12/18/19); Trump rails against impeachment

'She's losing her teeth,' Trumpty says,
Belittling our Speaker is par for this Prez.
When powerful women get in his way,
He needs to control them—or they'll rule the day.
Daily insults are hurled from this clown,
Congress, please ACT and take this guy down!

Re: Article—(WAPO) Trump campaign held a Halloween 'Witch Hunt Party' (10/31/19); other news sources: New York Daily News, eve of House impeachment, supporters hold 'Ding Dong, the witch is dead' party, vilifying Speaker Pelosi (12/17/19)

Trumpty says it's a 'total witch hunt,'
A 'perversion of justice,' a deliberate affront
To a Presidency he did not expect,
But one that Trumpty will fight to protect!

Re: Article—(WAPO) After voting to impeach, House Democrats say Senate 'must eliminate the threat' the President poses to our national security (1/18/20)

Trumpty's a National Security threat,
He needs to be out, but don't place your bet.
We've trusted him with our nuclear codes,
Heaven forbid—if the world explodes!

Re: Article—(WAPO) Don't let the defense fool you. This impeachment is all about corruption (1/31/20)

Trumpty claims he's the 'Chosen One,'
Deserving of our adulation.
He came to save US from disaster,
But daily creates more cracks in the plaster.
'I alone can fix it,' he brags,
But a house will fall when its structure sags.
He's bad for our country—a pretender, a ruse,
His removal? unlikely—Repubs will refuse.

Re: Article—(WAPO) Rep. Adam Schiff (D-CA) ends impeachment hearings with passionate plea for fair Senate trial (2/6/20); he calls out a medieval image first invoked by confidant of the Trump administration to serve as warning to Republicans not to cross Trump

Trumpty Dumpty gets madder than h*ll,
When impeachment proceedings do not bode him well.
'Shifty Schiff's head should be on a pike!'
'Then he will know what it is like
To be vilified, as I have been,'
"I've done nothing wrong!" I'll say it again.
'Impeachment's a hoax, a fake, and a lie!'
It got his attention—no one can deny.

Re: Article—(WAPO) President celebrates Senate acquittal (2/6/20); other news sources, CNN, Trump holds press conference in White House East Room with supporters, venting his anger and flouting news headline of 'Acquittal' See also The Cult of Trumpty, Hijacking the GOP and Trumpty's MO, Exact Revenge!

A spiteful Trumpty goes off the rails,
Venting about impeachment travails.
He doubles down on his innocence,
Unleashing a torrent of grievances.
The Dems are "vicious and mean," he says,
A meltdown by an unstable Prez?
He heaps on Repubs lavish praise,
Who bask in his fawning as if in a daze.
This mobster 'family' on East Room display,
Dare not cross him, or they'll rue the day.
It's Trumpty unfiltered—so horrible to see,
To those in his clutches—are you ever free?

Re: Article—(WAPO) Post-acquittal 'trial' for impeachment, Trump gets revenge (2/7/20); other news sources: CNN; Trump fires Lt. Col. Alexander Vindman (and brother) from White House staff along with Ambassador Gordon Sondland, as punishment for their testimony in House impeachment inquiry. See also The Revolving Door

Trumpty Dumpty exacts retribution,
He wants his revenge! (did he learn that from Putin?)
He's acting like a boss of the Mob,
His staff dare not cross him; they fear for their job.

'You're fired,' he says, 'I've had it with you!'
This sorry scene reeks of Pepe Le Pew.*
Who will go next? No doubt there'll be more,
With 'heads on a pike,' they are marched out the door.

*Disney Looney Tunes—a skunk

XI.

THE RUSSIANS ARE COMING!
2020 ELECTION

Re: Article—(WAPO) How Trump can win re-election (7/3/20)

Trumpty Dumpty is desperate to win,
Four more years in the White House again.
Past actions have shown, without hesitation,
That he is a master of self-preservation.
Trumpty, the King, wants to reign on,
Voters! Please act and get rid of this Con!

Re: Articles—(WAPO) Trump is counting on Russian help to get re-elected (5/6/19); (NYT) 'Nothing less than a civil war,' the far right see doom without Trump (12/18/19)

Trumpty Dumpty and Ruski pal Vlad,
Are plotting a way for the Dems to be had.
Guiliani, Pompeo, and Barr would be in
On a plan to ensure that Trumpty will win.

News, several sources: Trump must remain in power to stay out of prison; Trump could face criminal charges if he loses 2020 (12/9-21/19)

Trumpty Dumpty will see (seize) a new term,
Unless Dems can act to take out this worm.
Buttigieg, Biden, or Harris* could win,
To keep Trumpty out of the White House again.
This Prez is desperate and surely he knows,
If not re-elected, to prison he goes.

*Democratic candidates Mayor Pete Buttigieg, former VP Joe Biden, Sen. Kamala Harris (D-CA)

Re: Article—(WAPO) 'It kind of failed us': with eyes of world on Iowa, another hiccup in American democracy (2/4/20)

Trumpty gloats sarcastically,
At the Iowa caucus catastrophe.
"The system was rigged," he taunts with disdain,
It's momentum akin to a badly wrecked train.
Primaries—push on! I'm counting on you,
To identify someone who'll represent BLUE.

Re: Articles—(WAPO) Across divided nation, skepticism about impeachment (9/27/19); (NYT) Trump is mentally unfit, no exam needed (10/11/19)

Trumpty the Oaf is a monster indeed.
He rages and roars; he's unfit to lead!
Four years as our Prez is entirely too long,
Will we ever recover after he's gone?
We need to plan now before it's too late,
Voters, DO NOT let this oaf take on eight!

Re: Articles—(WAPO) How Trump and Sanders turned populist
rage into political power (3/2/20), eve of Super Tuesday primary

Bernie and Trumpty both speak their minds,
In an odd-couple way, they're two of a kind.
Imagine them in a circus clown car,
Ranting and waving – such barkers they are.
One from the left and one from the right,
Supporters will cheer them by day and by night.
Their final debate would be quite the show.
Nor sure I could watch – I'll have popcorn to go.

Re: Article—(NYT) The lessons of 2016 (2/1/20)

Trumpty is our Imposter-in-Chief,
We're stuck with him now; there's no fast relief.
We gave him four years, but that is TOO LONG,
Will we ever recover after he's gone?
People, I plead—we must do our part,
And vote this fraud out before any wars start!

Re: Articles—(WAPO) Trump presented with grim internal polling showing him losing to Biden (4/29/20); photo of a disturbed and exhausted Trump; (NYT) Trump campaign looks at Electoral map and doesn't like what it sees (6/3/20)

> *Trumpty Dumpty looks angry and sad,*
> *He knows his own polling is really quite bad.*
> *What can he do to rev up his base?*
> *He'll lie through his teeth just to save face.*
> *He sees a great win in 2020,*
> *But angry old Trumpty may well come up empty.*

Re: Article—(WAPO) Biden campaign attacks a Trump Social Security plan that doesn't exist (9/4/20); other news sources: CNN, Biden shows the qualities Trump lacks at CNN town hall (9/18/20)

> *Donnie Dumpty and Empathy Joe,*
> *Are two polar opposites; that we all know.*
> *They're on the debate stage; it's clear Biden cares,*
> *Dumpty doesn't; he openly glares.*
> *Will he stalk Biden? (we've seen that before)*
> *He may very well try to do it once more.*
> *But Biden won't stand for it; I'm sure of that,*
> *He'll be prepared for Dumpty's worn 'tact'.*
> *Watch Dumpty stumble—fall flat on his face,*
> *Effectively putting an end to this race.*

Re: Articles—(WAPO) Trump is angry about his poll numbers and he has very good reason to be (4/30/20); (WAPO) Trump's assault on election integrity forces question: what would happen if he refused to accept a loss? (7/23/20)

Trumpty Dumpty will sniff, snarl, and snort,
When election returns have him coming up short.
Who can contain him? He DOES NOT like to lose!
Will this finally drive him to hitting the booze?
Probably not—but he'll rage and he'll fight!
He WILL NOT go gentle in-to that good night. *

*Dylan Thomas

Re: Article—(WAPO) Trump uses Rose Garden press briefing for extended campaign-like attack on Biden (7/14/20); other news sources: Trump attacks Biden's son Hunter, Rep. Alexandria Ocasio-Cortez (D-NY), Sen. Bernie Sanders (I-VT); event becomes a Trump rally*

*Violation of the Hatch Act, that prohibits Federal employees from engaging in political activities

Trumpty is ablaze again,
Desperate for a campaign win.
Time is slipping by him fast!
The election's looming; he may not last.
The thought of losing ignites his ire,
Holy Moley—a five-alarm fire!
At a press briefing in the Rose Garden,
He goes after Biden—I beg your pardon?

The Prez's rage is out of control,
Driven by a declining poll.
On Trumpty's face—an onerous scowl,
And from this garden—an odor most foul.
Campaign promises? not to be,
His 'rallies' are failing miserably.

Re: Article (WAPO) We've never backed a Democrat for president, but Trump must be defeated (4/15/20); The Lincoln Project Republicans* speak out: We are in extraordinary times

*George Conway, Jennifer Horn, Steve Schmidt, John Weaver, Rick Wilson, others

Listen up, Trumpty, I'm telling you,
Our country is turning a bright shade of blue.
An electoral win is in jeopardy,
As voters head off aristocracy.
Arizona is likely to register blue,
Led by Tucsonans (I know quite a few).
Colorado, Nevada, and places far west,
Will put their 'old red' to a 'new blue' test.

Local (Arizona) take: Article—(WAPO) Sen. Martha McSally (R-AZ) slams reporter as 'liberal hack' and Trump 2020 offers fundraising boost (1/16/20)

AZ 2020 Prediction

Arizona will take on a new blue hue,
Led by Tucsonans—they know what to do.

Martha McSally is on her way out,
Mark Kelly* will win! I have no doubt.
Up north, Joe Arpaio will be out the door,
Quoth The Raven, "Nevermore."**

*Democratic Senate candidate (and former astronaut) Mark Kelly
**Edgar Allan Poe

Re: Article—(WAPO) Arizona GOP says it will stop Mark Kelly "dead in his tracks"* (9/6/19)

*Quote from Republican Party Chairwoman, Kelli Ward

Putin's Don and Chemtrails* Kelli,
Are doomed in this state, come 2020.
We'll vote out a failed, corrupt GOP.
Mark Kelly will WIN; just wait and see!

*Ward called out a secret government plan (unproven) of environmental pollution from chemicals emitted by airplanes' vapor emissions (contrails), during 2018 primary bid for John McCain's Senate seat

In 2020 for our Nation's Sake

Dump Trump—into a Slump
  (a raging one no doubt—from which he won't easily recover)
Punch Pence—into a Fence
  (outfitted with concertina wire—aka Nogales?)*
Pitch Mitch—into a Ditch
  (filled with fellow swampy crocs/crooks and h*ssing snakes)
A fitting fate for those who fan hate,
It's OUR action to take before it's too late.
How long can we wait?

*Twin border communities—Nogales, AZ and Nogales, Sonora (Mexico)

XII

HEALTH HAZARDS AHEAD

Mental (un)Fitness for Office
(Sociopathic Characteristics)

Angry, Raging

Trumpty's like a hot air balloon,
Expanding with rage, he'll explode very soon.
Watch him inflate; at some point he'll burst,
The cleanup for US will be some of the worst!
Fragments of Trumpty soon cover the town,
So grab your keepsakes as they rain down.

Callous, Cruel

Trumpty Dumtpy couldn't care less,
He doesn't connect with souls under stress.
He has no compassion for suffering of others,
Certainly not for Gold Star mothers.*
Nor Puerto Ricans after their flood,
Nor people of Houston, when knee-deep in mud.

The list goes on; he just doesn't care,
Empathy? Zero—it's simply not there.

*Gold Star mother, Ghazala Khan whose son, U.S. Army Captain H. Kahn, was killed in Iraq

Chaotic, Indecisive, Impulsive

Trumpty Dumpty blows in the wind,
One day he's out; the next day he's in.
He'll convince us he's made a red-line decision,
But later we find it's up for revision.

Corollary I

Trumpty Dumpty walks back a decision,
There's a history of actions up for revision.
He exhausts US with chaos; he wants to confuse,
To Trumpty, is it all just a big ruse?

Corollary II

Trumpty acts according to whim,
Decisions are made to benefit HIM.
He governs on impulse; can we not see?
There's no long-range planning—as there should be.
Is he working for US—or some foreign state?
We need to know before it's too late.

Re: Article—(NYT) Trump's tactic; sowing distrust in whatever gets in his way (9/3/20)

Trumpty, our Disrupter-in-Chief,
Sows doubt and distrust to the point of grief!
We should not rely on a word that he says,
It's time to be rid of this unstable Prez.

Deceitful

See All the President's Lies!

Delusional, Deranged

Trumpty Dumpty distorts the truth,
When confronted with facts, he'll say, 'there's no proof.'
His beliefs become 'truths' for whatever he says,
The MO* of a delusional Prez.

*Modus Operandi

Trump lives in a made-up reality,
It's a fantasy kingdom the whole world can see.
'Alternative facts' should sound an alarm!
His lie-based decisions can cause US much harm.

Donnie Quixote dreams bigly, for sure,
He chases fake dreams and windmills that whirr...
In his 'tilting of windmills' he dreams of a WIN,
And rides forth to battle the demons within.

See also The Great (non)Communicator, The (mis)Spoken Word

Egotistical, Narcissistic

Trumpty's in love with his reflection,
He looks at himself and sees perfection.
His image in the Reflecting Pool,*
Speaks back to him, 'You're just SO COOL!'

*Reflecting Pool on the National Mall

Ignorant, Illiterate

Trumpty displays a fragile ego,
That stems from his childhood long ago.
He craves recognition; can we not see?
A rejection will wound him, though not fatally.
Trumpty will fight! His ego must WIN,
As he keeps playing US again and again.

Trumpty Dumpty is unfit to lead,
A disgrace to his office; he barely can read!
Our Constitution is 'over his head,'
He can't comprehend what Madison* said.
The Bill of Rights makes little sense,
Trump's cognitive skills are frightfully dense.

*James Madison, 4th President of the United States and a framer of U.S. Constitution

Re: Article—(WAPO) Trump's photo-op play: facing impeachment, the president strives to look hard at work (11/30/19); claimed 'he opened' factory that has been producing Apple MacPros since 2012; signed several bills before leaving for Thanksgiving vacation and made surprise visit to troops in Afghanistan

Trumpty Dumpty calls it a day,
"Working my a** off" in his self-serving way.
He opened a factory; he signed a new bill,
He visited troops to please those on The Hill.
Trumpty's a braggart; he boasts mostly for show,
He wants recognition; that we well know.

Re: (WAPO podcast) Highlighting new book, *A Very Stable Genius* by Carol Leonnig and Philip Rucker, (1/24/20), a first-hand account of Trump's visit to the Pentagon for a security briefing

Trumpty visits the Pentagon's Tank,
For a classified briefing from persons with rank.
Generals and aides try their level best,
To impart some history, but Trump's not impressed.
"There's not enough winning—you're losers," he says.
An insensitive sting from this arrogant Prez!
Tillerson* watches as Trumpty implodes,
(And we've given this guy our nuclear codes?)
"You're a bunch of dopes and babies," Trump rants,
Give this Prez a kick in the pants!
Or simply remove him—Congress can ACT,
Our Constitution provides for that.

*Rex Tillerson, Secretary of State

Infantile

Re: Article—(WAPO) Trump reacts to confrontation from Speaker Pelosi at a Cabinet meeting (10/17/19); other news sources: iconic photo—our Speaker stands and wags finger at Trump (Pelosi later sends out photo on Twitter); Trump is taken aback, annoyed, angered

Trumpty Dumpty calls a meeting,
His Cabinet is present; some begin tweeting.
Speaker Pelosi confronts our Prez,
"Do all roads lead to Putin?" She sharply says.

Trumpty recoils and calls her 'third-rate,'
He can't disguise his slow-boiling hate.
Look at his face—the pouting frown,
Our Toddler-in-Chief in total meltdown.

Re: Article—(WAPO) Trump's extraordinary Oval Office squabble with Senate Minority Leader Chuck Schumer (D-NY) and House Speaker Nancy Pelosi (D-CA) (12/11/18); all exchange sharp words

Trumpty Dumpty, Toddler-in-Chief,
Throws tantrums and hissy's beyond belief!
Who is to stop him with no mom nearby?
Nancy can't do it, although she may try.
The toddler is playing US; will we let him win?
It's past time for Congress to rein this Prez in!

Re: Article—(WAPO) Trump's sweeping rebuttal to Sondland's* testimony (11/20/19); quoting his own denials of Quid Pro Quo (Ukraine scandal), Trump reads hand-lettered note—large letters written with a Sharpie See also The Great (non)Communicator, Forecaster-in-Chief

*Ambassador Gordon Sondland, testifying in House impeachment inquiry

Trumpty is a Simpleton,
A child with his Sharpie pen.
Unfitness for the Presidency,
Displayed in ink for the world to see.

Manipulative

Re: Article—(WAPO) From Access Hollywood to Russia... (11/28/17); other news sources: Trump's extremely lewd remarks during an interview could have, but did not, doom his election

> *Trumpty claims he is a star,*
> *When you're a celeb, that's what you are.*
> *He brags he'd never be a wussy,*
> *Afraid to grab 'em by the p*ssy.*
> *"They let you do it"; it's so easy,*
> *Spare US, please! The man is sleazy.*

Re: Article—(NYT) The politics of exhaustion (12/12/19); other news sources: Trump and the media -Trump relies on and controls the Press; being constantly on camera is a win for Trump

> *Trump is a clown show we watch every day,*
> *Spinning the news in his self-absorbed way.*
> *How do we avoid him? (not easy to do)*
> *Trump pollutes airwaves like Pepe Le Pew.**
> *Try changing the channel? He just reappears,*
> *It's useless to try to adjust rabbit ears.*
> *Voters, please help get this guy off TV,*
> *The Trump Show must end—for ETERNITY.*

*Disney Looney Tunes—a skunk

Physical (un)Fitness for Office

News: Early in Presidency, Trump undergoes examination by White House physician, Dr. Ronny Jackson, who declares the President in good health

Trumpty Dumpty visits his Doc,
To see if his heart beats a steady 'tic-toc.'
Your pulse is amazing! That's good news for you,
I'll note you're a most stable genius, too.
But I caution: go easy on burgers and fries,
You'll want to avoid an early demise.
Here's a tweet from Melania: 'Might it Be Best
To schedule for Donnie a Rorschach* test?'
'I'm concerned that he's not mentally well,'
'Lately, I feel I'm living in h*ll.'
(No worries Ma'm—I'll take care of it for you,
I too have concerns that his brain is askew.)
That's all for today, and you're free to go,
If you have any questions, please let me know.
Some final notes to put in my log:
'Empathy lacking; recommend dog.'

*Rorschach inkblot imaging test used in assessment of psychological functioning

Re: Article—(WAPO) Only cauliflower can save us now—Trump's eating patterns and preferences (2/27/20); other news sources: CNN, Trump dines in open setting at Mar-a-Lago with China's President and discusses bombing of a Syrian airstrip (classifed info) while sharing "the most beautiful piece of chocolate cake" (4/13/17); Trump demands two scoops of ice cream with his dessert (guests are served one scoop) (5/1/17)

Trumpty Dumpty is bigly obese,
His diet must be hard to police.
He gobbles down burgers and fries and Cokes,
Stuffing himself, he nearly chokes.
His chocolate cake is most renown,
Some say, 'the most beautiful cake' in town!
A day WILL come when he exits the door,
With ice cream* to go as a souvenir.

*2 scoops

XIII.

VIRUS CRISIS!
(SAD SAGA OF FAILED LEADERSHIP)

Re: Articles—(WAPO) Trump can't handle a crisis he didn't create (3/7/20); (WAPO) Besieged Trump announces Europe travel ban in effort to stem coronavirus pandemic (3/11/20); (NYT) The President as bystander: Trump struggles to unify a nation on edge (3/12/20)

Trumpty comes up with the perfect plan,
To hide the Corona as long as he can.
He'll fool the public; don't you see?
*He says he knows more than the CDC.**
I've "maybe a natural ability,"
To understand science to a tee.
People are dying in plain sight,
As he smugly assures US all will be right.
A failure of leadership from this Prez!
Can anyone trust a word that he says?

*Centers for Disease Control and Prevention

Re: Articles—(WAPO) Without guidance from the top, Americans have been left to figure out their own Coronavirus solutions (3/15/20); (NYT) CDC gives new guidelines, New York to close restaurants and schools, and Italian deaths rise (3/15/20)

'Beware the Ides of March,'* we recall,

As Covid-19 consumes US all.

We dare not gather as we please,

In fear of a hiccup, a cough, or a sneeze.

We're greeted by knuckle-bump, elbow, or boot,

In some cases maybe a formal salute.

Lives are on hold across our great nation,

As we wait for an end to this strange infestation.

*Shakepeare's *Julius Caesar*

Re: Articles—(WAPO) "I ran the White House Pandemic Office. Trump closed it"* (3/13/20); (WAPO) Trump melts down and the media fails the public. Again (3/19/20); other news sources: CNN, White House press briefing: Trump dismisses question from a female NPR reporter

*Beth Cameron, WH National Security Council Directorate for Global Health Security; office closed in 2018

Trumpty Dumpty calls in the Press,

For an update on the Coronavirus.

A reporter seeks an answer that's candid,

On why the Pandemic Office disbanded.

Such "a nasty question," he said.

See the Press Corp shudder with dread.

"I take no responsibility," Trumpty retorts defiantly.
No empathy from this self-proclaimed 'King,'
Of people's on-going suffering.
'We're doing a great job," is what he'll say,
He ends all discussion and calls it a day.

News, several sources: CNN, Trump holds press conference to give update on the supply chain for medical equipment, such as masks and ventilators, to meet Coronavirus demands (3/20/20); takes questions from the Press

Re: Articles—(WAPO) Trump's eruption at NBC reporter underscores his 'alternate reality' on virus (3/20/20); (NYT) Trump resists pressure to use wartime law (Defense Production Act) to mobilize industry in virus response (3/20/20)

Trumpty Dumpty is under duress,
During a briefing on the Coronavirus.
"We'll have millions of masks—very soon," he says,
A false assurance from this Prez?
We're "being besieged in a beautiful way
By companies." (who will help save the day?)
A reporter notes that people are scared,
What would he do to assure them he cared.
Our Prez takes offense and then goes BERSERK!
The crowd is aghast (this guy is a jerk)!
"You're a terrible reporter—that's what I say,"
It's "a nasty question," by the way.
Doc Fauci,* thank goodness, sets everyone straight,
To be 'prepared fully,' we have a long wait.
Trumpty scowls at being contradicted,
Top LEADERSHIP MISSING; we might have predicted.

*Dr. Anthony S. Fauci, Director, National Institute of Allergy and Infectious Diseases

Re: Article—(WAPO) Image (hand-written notes with change marked) highlights Trump's deliberate tag of 'Chinese' to characterize Coronavirus (3/19/20)

> *Trumpty Dumpty amends his notes,*
> *With supporters in mind? (he needs their votes)*
> *He marks out 'Corona' and pencils 'Chinese,'*
> *A racist labeling of this disease?*
> *He revels in calling this virus 'Kung Flu,'*
> *It's classic Trumpty; it's what he will do.*
> *He turns to name-calling, like in his campaign,*
> *His MO is finding someone to blame!*

Re: Article—(WAPO) A President with no empathy exploits the Coronavirus (3/23/20); other news sources: Trump holds daily press conferences on Coronavirus; acts like he's campaigning; praises himself for the good job he's doing; calls himself the 'Wartime President' and rambles about spending millions to get elected

> *Trumpty says he's the 'Wartime Prez,'*
> *"I'm doing a great job," or so he says.*
> *By mobilizing the DPA,**
> *Masks and vents should come quickly our way.*
> *We'll practice 'social distancing,'*
> *He's told this should work, but is not a sure thing.*
> *"We're at war" fighting an enemy,*
> *A foreign invader we cannot see.*
> *But for weeks he dismissed this serious threat,*
> *'Twill be "gone by spring" was his sure bet.*

He hears of Mitt Romney's self-quarantine,
"Gee, that's too bad." (good—Mitt won't be seen)
(Nor heard from either)—OK by Trump,
Since Mitt** was on board with his impeachment.
"I love being your Prez" and spent "millions to get here,"
Our lack of a leader has never been clearer.
This 'Wartime Prez' really must go!
It's now up to voters to cancel the show.

*Defense Production Act
**Senator Mitt Romney (R-UT) voted to convict in impeachment trial

News, several sources: Trump slams Gov. Gretchen Whitmer's response to Federal assistance for masks and ventilators, saying she doesn't 'appreciate' what he's done for her State; tells VP Mike Pence "not to call the woman in Michigan" (3/27/20)

Trumpty trashes perceived enemies,
Hitting back hard when they fail to please.
He denigrates Michigan's Governor,*
When he gets 'no appreciation' from her.
He helped her State find needed supplies,
A praise-worthy gesture in Trumpty's eyes.
If someone annoys him, he can't let it go,
A character flaw? undoubtedly so.
That shouldn't excuse him; but what can we do?
Come 2020, we all MUST VOTE BLUE.

*Gov. Gretchen Whitmer (D-MI)

Re: Article—(NYT) Testing blunders cost.....(3/29/20); other news sources: Speaker Pelosi talks to Jake Tapper on MSNBC's State of the Union—Trump's actions on Coronavirus to date have been inadequate (3/29/20); (NYT) Testing blunders cost vital month in U.S. virus fight (3/29/20)

"As our President fiddles, people are dying,"
Pelosi* responds to a national out-crying.
There's a shortage of masks, ventilators, and beds,
Inaction is tearing our hopes into shreds.
Three D's of disaster, repeated here,
'Denial, Delay, Deadly'—for sure.
Impeachment? Our Congress will not be swayed,
The coming Election MUST NOT be delayed!

*House Speaker Nancy Pelosi (D-CA)—the 3 D's of failure to take action

Re: Article—(WAPO) "I know we feel under attack," Gov. Cuomo tells New Yorkers rattled by quarantine talks (3/29/20) See also Health Hazards Ahead—Mental (un)Fitness, Chaotic, Indecisive, Impulsive

Trumpty Dumpty zigs and zags,
With the novel Corona, he runs into snags.
He says he'll quarantine three Northeast States,
Then changes his mind on action he'll take.
Missing is strong Federal oversight,
He fights with Cuomo,* who tries to do right.
With an indecisive Trumpty at play,
We're left counting the days 'til Election Day.

*Gov. Andrew Cuomo (D-NY)

Re: Articles—(WAPO) Inside the Coronavirus testing failure: alarm and dismay among scientists who sought to help (4/3/20); (WAPO) As testing outcry mounts, Trump cedes to states in announcing guidelines for slow reopening (4/16/20); (WAPO) How Trump has shifted his rhetoric on coronavirus testing (4/17/20)

Trumpty Dumpty plays down the tests,
For the novel Coronavirus.
Where are the masks? Where is the testing?
We can't curb the spread without investing
In test kits and centers to carry this out.
A failure to use Executive clout?
He dismisses the threat—'twill be gone by spring,'
But who knows what the summer will bring?
His failure to lead—so sad to see,
Tests our very Democracy.

News, several sources: The Guardian, ABC, Trump dismisses wearing mask, although CDC recommends it; says he greets kings, queens, ambassadors, dictators behind the Resolute Desk—how would that look? (4/5/20)

Trumpty Dumpty won't wear a mask,
In defiance of what the CDC asks.
'It's optional,' and 'I'm not going to do it,'
He doubles down hard and is most resolute.
'It's voluntary—don't ask me again,'
'How would I look greeting a King?'
It's all about HIM; what can we do?
Come 2020, we will VOTE BLUE.

Corollary

Trumpty says he's come around,
To wearing a mask. (he's quite the clown)
"I like the way I look in a mask,"
What did he say? We dare not ask.
Trump likens himself to the 'Lone Ranger,'*
Who rode to protect the country from danger.
In wearing a mask like his cowboy hero,
He pretends he can lead, while fiddling like Nero.**

*Sole survivor of ambushed Texas Rangers, who rode to establish law and order
**Claudius Nero, Emperor of Rome, 54-68 A.D., said to have fiddled while Rome burned

Re: Articles—(WAPO) Trump's comments prompt doctors, and Lysol, to warn against injecting disinfectants (4/24/20); (WAPO) 13 Hours of Trump: President fills press briefings with attacks and boasts (4/26/20)

Trumpty Dumpty's at it again,
He's our nation's premier Medicine Man.
Hawking a cure for Covid-19,
Sunlight and bleach. (that remains to be seen)
An injection of Lysol is just what you need,
One quick prick; you won't even bleed.
Or just "hit the body…with powerful light,"
'It'll kill the virus,' and all will be right.
"Maybe you can and maybe you can't,"
"I'm not a doctor," he goes on to rant.

*"I'm a person who has a good you-know-what,"**
O spare US—please! enough of this rot!

*pointing to his brain

Re: Articles—(NYT) He could have seen what was coming: behind Trump's failure on the virus (4/11/20); (WAPO) Pathetic displays like these are all Trump has left (4/16/20)

Trumpty Dumpty has now become,
Pathetic Trumpty, in more ways than one.
His handling of a deadly virus,
Put US to shame; he lost our trust.
Trumpty expressed no great alarm,
For this pandemic early on.
News of its spread was a national nightmare,
Masks and vents—we were desperate to share.
He wasted time by twiddling his thumbs,
Supplies go abroad and we're left with the crumbs.
A fool in charge of our nation's well-being,
How this turns out remains to be seen.
Pathetic Trumpty deserves his fate,
2020 for him? Too little, too late.

Re: Article—(NYT) 'Scary to Go to Work': White House races to contain virus in its ranks (5/10/20); (WAPO) White House aides rattled after positive coronavirus tests and officials send mixed messages on how to respond (5/10/20)

Trumpty Dumpty coughs and spouts,
It's the dreaded Covid-19, no doubt.
It invaded the White House, perhaps to stay,
Oh, "it will be gone" within a day.
Trumpty's at risk, can we not see?
And so is our nation, indefinitely.

As he struggles to calm US, options are few,
'Out, out damned spot!'* be gone with you!

*Shakespeare's Macbeth

News, several sources: CNN, White House press conference—announcement of administration's Operation Warp Speed* (5/1/20)

*Ref., *Star Trek*

Trumpty Dumpty's on a roll,
'Op Warp Speed' is his new goal.
A quick vaccine is what we need,
Developed at tremendous speed.
With Trumpty oversight? He's THE MAN.
"Who's in charge of it? Honest(ly) I am."
Problem solved! We are good to go.
If Trumpty wills it—it is so!

Re: Articles—(WAPO) Poll finds universal lifestyle changes, stress and growing fears about catching coronavirus (3/27/20); (NYT) He could have seen what was coming: behind Trump's failure on the virus (4/11/20); (WAPO) As virus takes hold, resistance to stay-at-home orders remains widespread—exposing political and social rifts (4/14/20)

We can thank this terrible pandemic for one thing:

To help US save our Democracy,
A virus will bring down this Presidency.

XIV

ALL GOOD THINGS MUST COME TO AN END

Trumpty Dumpty sat high on his wall,
But Covid-19 was his downfall.
All his supporters and all his henchmen,
Couldn't put Trumpty in power again.

Final thoughts on The Trump Error:

We exist in a perpetual fog,
Can we ever hope to drain the bog?*
I'm clueless like the slow-boiling frog,
Croaking away as I end my log.

*aka Trump's 'swamp'

THE END

APPENDIX

I submitted my first comment, a limerick, early in 2017 in response to an article in the New York Times on the confirmation of Scott Pruitt as Secretary of the Environmental Protection Agency (EPA). The poem reads:

We mourn our good earth under Pruitt,
Whose mantra has been to pollute it.
'Now take that you Feds!
I'll destroy all your Regs!'
'You gave me permission to do it.'

More about rhythm and meter:

Iambic meter is a rhythmic structure of poetry, consisting of an unstressed syllable and a stressed syllable, or an 'iamb.' Iambic refers to 'foot' or metric measure. The most common rhythms are iambic pentameter (five stressed syllables) and iambic tetrameter (four stressed syllables). William Shakespeare favored iambic pentameter in writing his sonnets, as did Geoffrey Chaucer in his *Canterbury Tales*. American poet Robert Frost's *Stopping by the Woods on a Snowy Evening* is an example of iambic tetrameter: 'taDUH, taDUH, taDUH, taDUH', as in 'Whose WOODS these ARE, I DO not KNOW; his HOUSE is IN the VILLage THOUGH,' and

'My LITtle HORSE must THINK it QUEER; to STOP withOUT a FARMhouse NEAR.' Another example: iambic trimeter '- a verse of three metic units, as in 'we SEE, we HEAR, we KNOW; the WAY that WE must GO.'

Most of my Trumpty rhymes are a mix of the 'DUHta' and 'taDUH,' stressed and unstressed syllables, often with 'pickup' notes, as in

TRUMPty DUMPty HASn't a CLUE,
(DUHta DUHta DUHta taDUH)
He's LIKE the old WOman who LIVED in a SHOE,
('ta' DUHta 'ta' DUHta 'ta' DUHta taDUH)

Poetry does not need to rhyme nor does it have to adhere to a metric pattern. Many poems are written in "Free Verse," an artistic expression evoking imagery and emotion.

See the Introduction for further discussion of rhythm, meter and poetic structure.

ABOUT THE AUTHOR

 Valerie Anderson was born in Denver, CO and grew up in Northeast Iowa near the scenic Upper Mississippi River Valley bordering Wisconsin and Minnesota. She attended Drake University, majoring in English while taking elective music courses. After receiving her Bachelor of Liberal Arts, she taught English in an Iowa high school. After moving with her husband to Cambridge, MA, she was a staff assistant for two years at the Harvard Graduate School of Education's Programmed Instruction Library, assisting with acquisitions and maintaining the collection. She later studied organ and music theory at Stephens College in Columbia, MO. In pursuing an interest in design, she earned a Bachelor of Architecture degree from the University of Tennessee, Knoxville.

Anderson spent a rewarding twenty-five-plus-year career as a technical writer/project manager in Oak Ridge, TN as a contractor for the Department of Energy (DOE). Her work at the Oak Ridge Institute for Science and Education (ORISE) included responsibility for DOE's Office of Health, Safety, and Security's complex-wide Security Awareness Special Interest Group (SASIG), coordinating workshops and developing guidance for National Security briefings. She served as project manager for a *DOE Marking Handbook,*

detailing document-marking requirements for various levels of classified and (unclassified) sensitive information. Under DOE's Work for Others program, she coauthored a *DOD Marking Guide* for the Department of Defense's (DOD) Technical Information Center, and developed materials and reports for other government agencies, including the Nuclear Regulatory Commission and the Centers for Disease Control and Prevention.

About the Illustrator

Arnie Bermudez is a Latino artist and cartoonist from southern Arizona. He has been drawing and poking fun at life ever since he could hold a pencil. He is available for freelance illustration work and caricatures in political cartoon style artwork.

Born and raised by a field worker and cleaning lady in Yuma, AZ, Arnie graduated from the University of Arizona with a Bachelor of Fine Arts degree. He lives in Tucson and has worked for the *Tucson Citizen* as their cartoonist. His work has appeared in the *Tucson Citizen*, the *Tucson Weekly*, FoxNewsLatino.com, TucsonSentinel.com and blogforarizona.net.

CPSIA information can be obtained
at www.ICGtesting.com
Printed in the USA
FSHW010607071020
74527FS